ROBERT D. VANDALL'S
FAVORITE SOLOS
12 OF HIS ORIGINAL PIANO SOLOS

FOREWORD

Each year Alfred publishes a variety of sheet music solos and individual collections for students at various levels. Teachers and students use them for recitals, auditions, festivals, or just to have fun. Many of these become student favorites, and teachers continue to teach them through the years.

Just as teachers and students have their own preferences, the composers who write these solos also have their personal favorites. For the Composer's Choice series, the editors at Alfred asked each composer to choose his or her best-loved solos that have been published throughout their careers, and compile them into graded collections for students. Each composer reflected on the inspiration, emotion, and memories behind their pieces that had brought so much joy to countless students and teachers.

As a result of this process, Alfred is pleased to introduce Robert D. Vandall's *Favorite Solos*, Book 2, a collection of twelve early intermediate to intermediate solos for students of all ages. Students, teachers, and audiences will enjoy the variety of styles, sounds, and moods of this music. We feel sure that Robert's *Favorite Solos* will quickly become your favorites, too. Enjoy!

CONTENTS

Alfred Music
P.O. Box 10003
Van Nuys, CA 91410-0003
alfred.com

ISBN-10: 0-7390-9350-9
ISBN-13: 978-0-7390-9350-4

Barnstorm Boogie

(from *Images*)

Robert D. Vandall

Walking Home

Robert D. Vandall

*Optional: swing the 8th notes

Another Spring

Robert D. Vandall

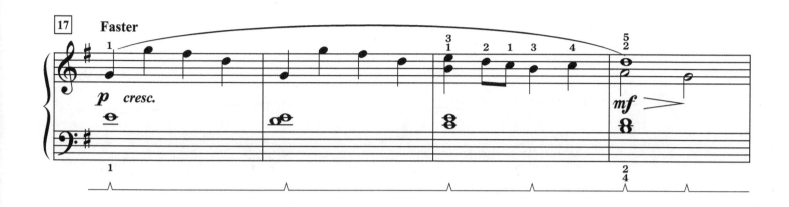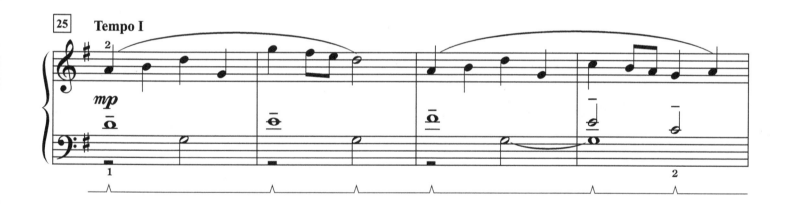

A Special Day

Robert D. Vandall

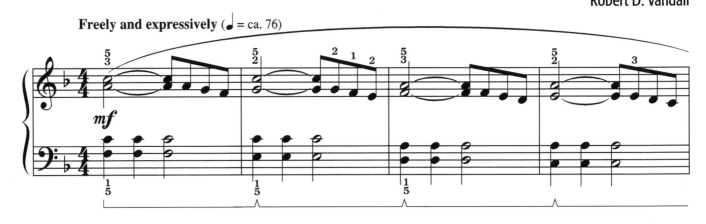

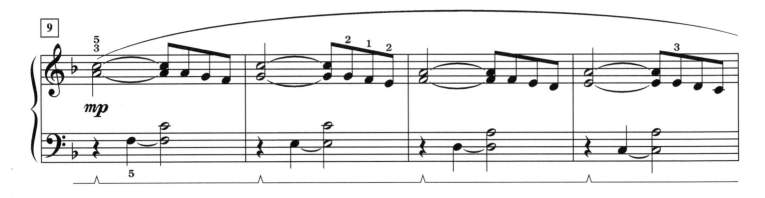

9

Rocky Mountain Morning

Robert D. Vandall

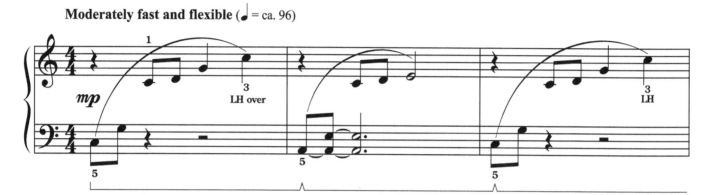

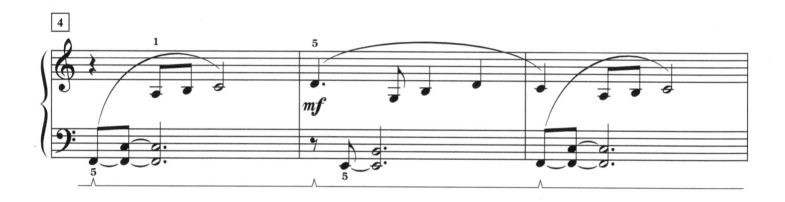

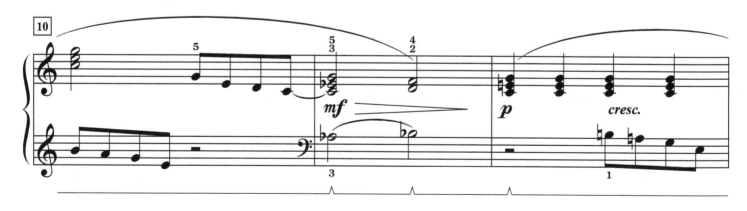

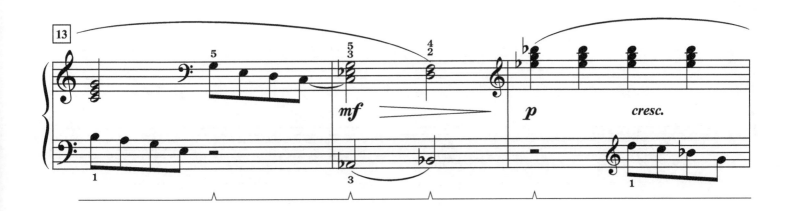

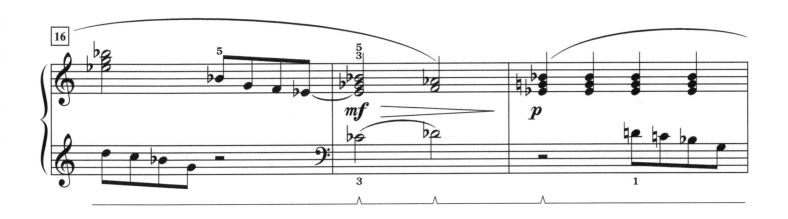

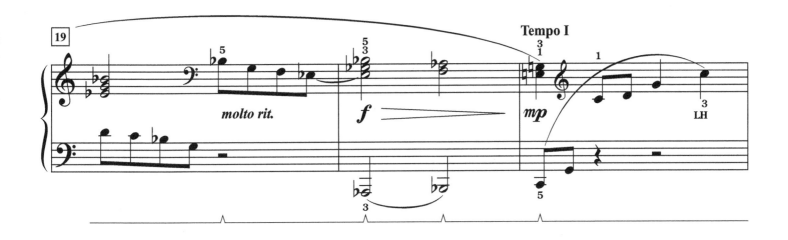

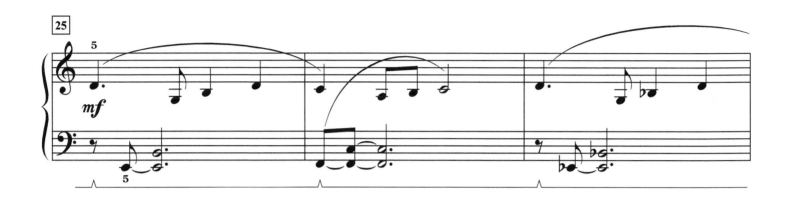

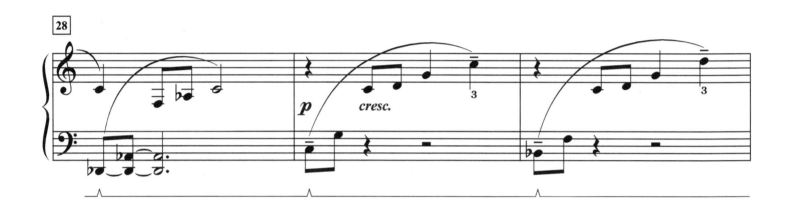

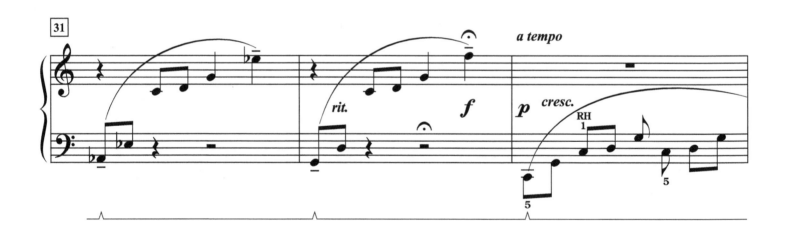

Dedicated to the National Guild of Piano Teachers of Marion, Ohio,
in honor of the 50th Anniversary of their center (1958–2008)

Reflections

Robert D. Vandall

Moderately fast, with much flexibility (♩ = ca. 96)

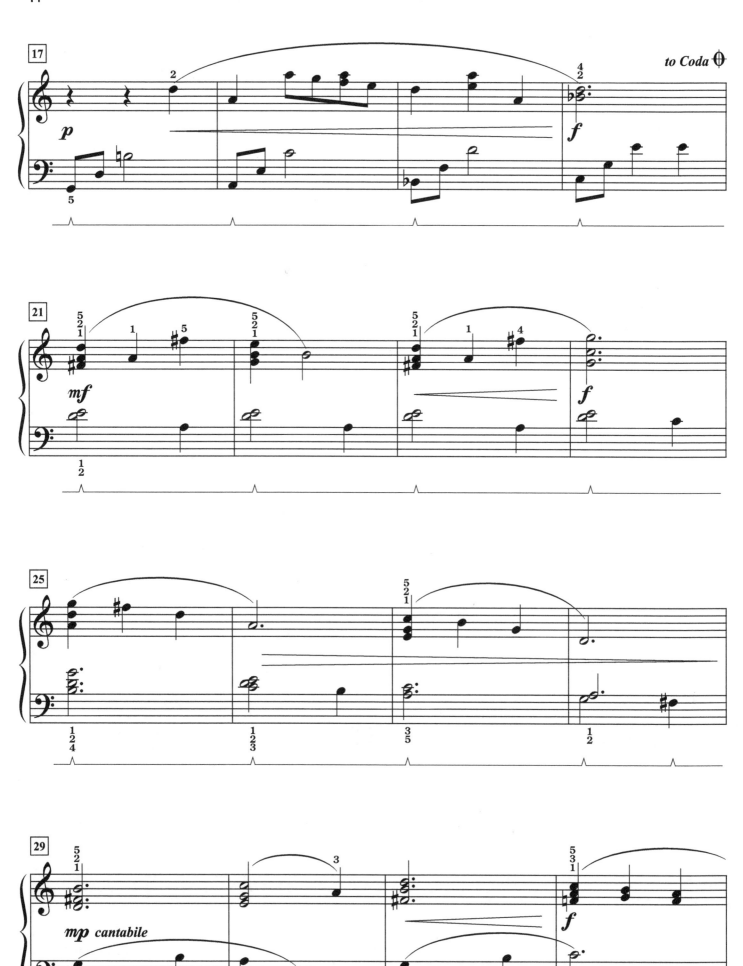

to Coda

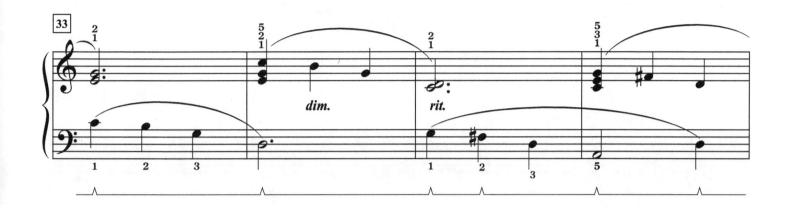

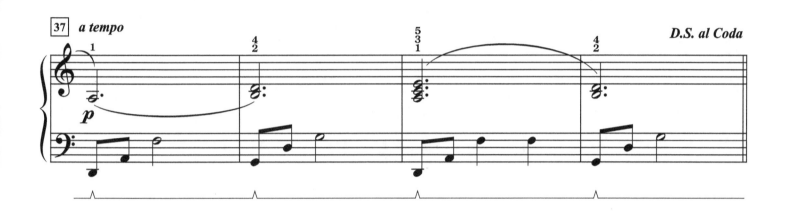

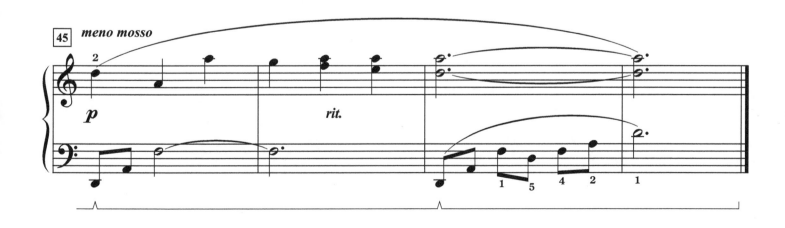

Hungarian Dance

(from *Romantic Inspirations*)

Robert D. Vandall

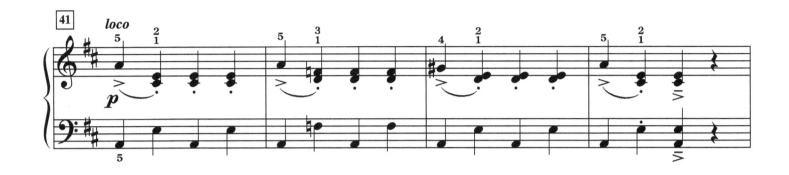

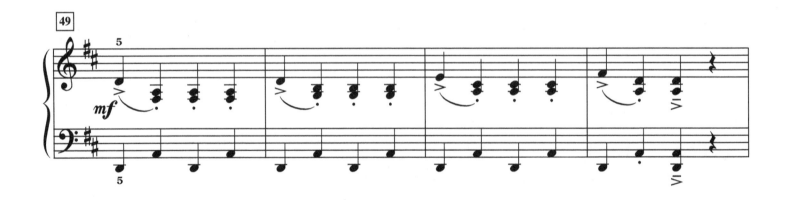

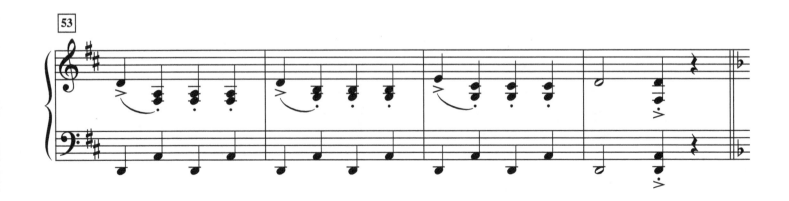

Summer Toccatina

(from *Short Suite*)

Robert D. Vandall

Bagatelle No. 17

(from *Bagatelles, Book 2*)

Robert D. Vandall

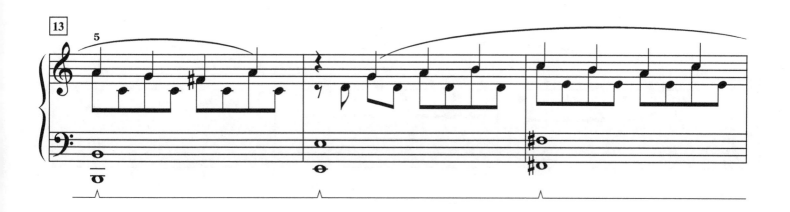

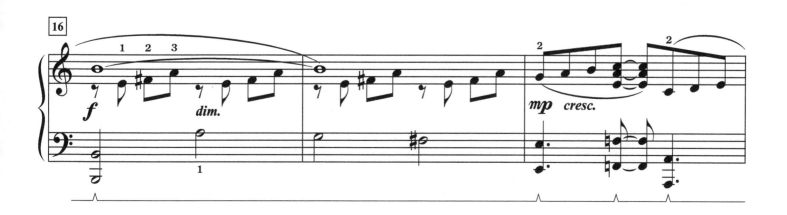

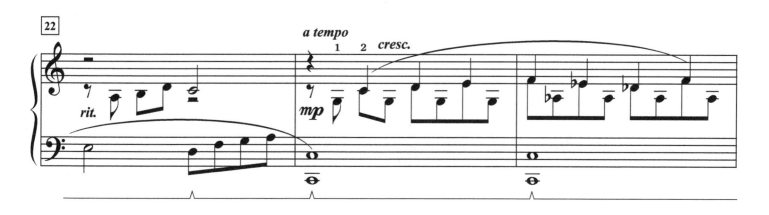

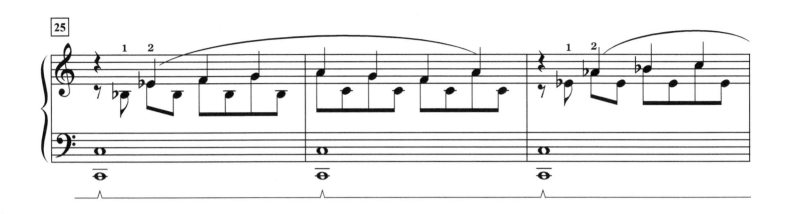

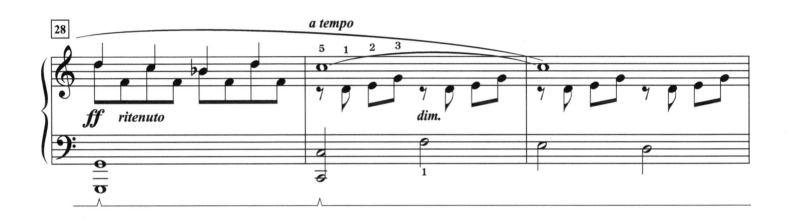

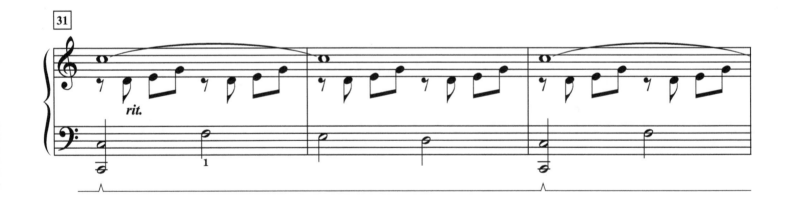

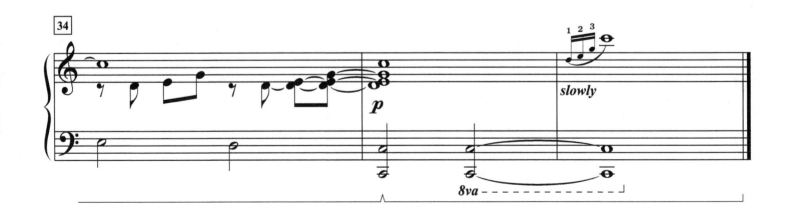

Bagatelle No. 19

(from *Bagatelles, Book 2*)

Robert D. Vandall

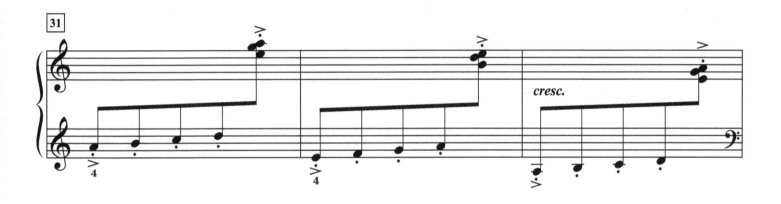

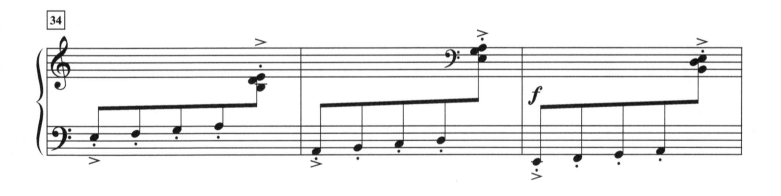

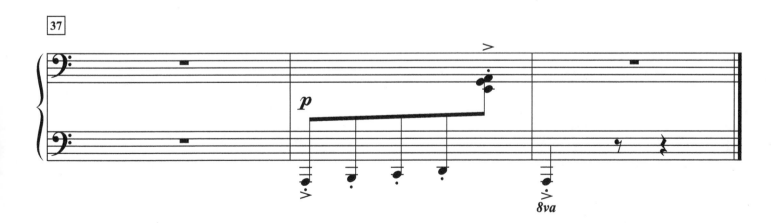

Etude No. 1 in F Major

(from *Etude Suite*)

Robert D. Vandall

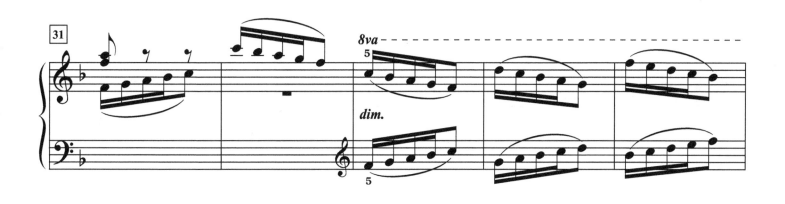

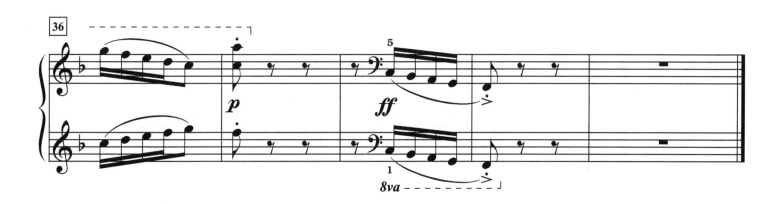

Triaditude

Robert D. Vandall

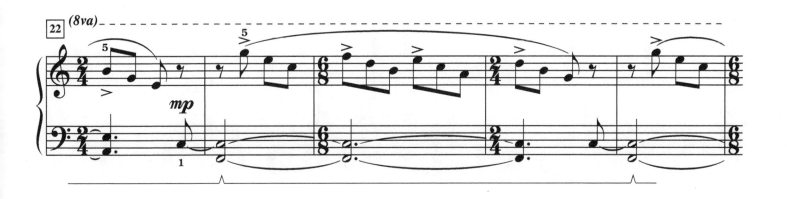

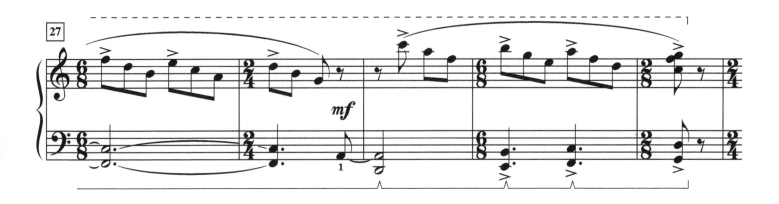

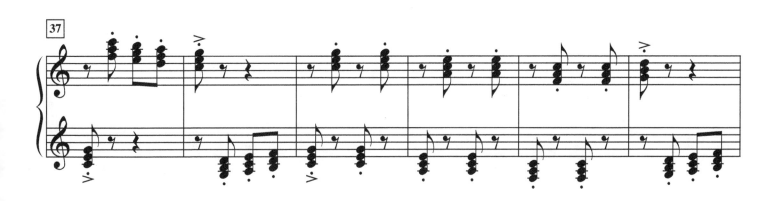

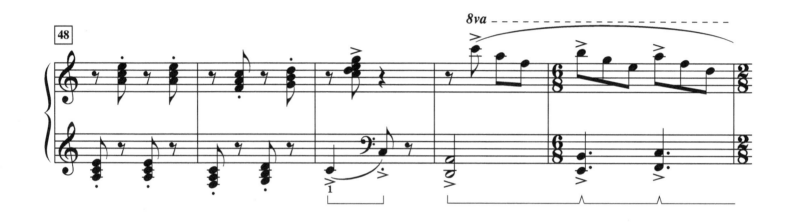